Piano • Vocal • Guitar

THE ULTIMATE

ELTON JOHN

COLLECTION

Volume Two

ISBN 0-7935-9409-X

HAL•LEONARD®
CORPORATION
7777 W. BLUEMOUND RD. P.O. BOX 13819 MILWAUKEE, WI 53213

Visit Hal Leonard Online at
www.halleonard.com

CONTENTS

SONG	FIRST APPEARED ON THIS ALBUM:
152 SKYLINE PIGEON	*Empty Sky* (1975)
139 SLEEPING WITH THE PAST	*Sleeping with the Past* (1989)
158 SOMEONE SAVED MY LIFE TONIGHT	*Captain Fantastic and the Brown Dirt Cowboy* (1975)
162 SOMETHING ABOUT THE WAY YOU LOOK TONIGHT	*The Big Picture* (1997)
168 SONG FOR GUY	*A Single Man* (1978)
172 SORRY SEEMS TO BE THE HARDEST WORD	*Blue Moves* (1976)
176 STEP INTO CHRISTMAS	*To Be Continued* (1990)
183 SWEET PAINTED LADY	*Goodbye Yellow Brick Road* (1973)
186 TAKE ME TO THE PILOT	*Elton John* (1970)
189 TEACHER I NEED YOU	*Don't Shoot Me I'm Only the Piano Player* (1973)
194 TINY DANCER	*Madman Across the Water* (1971)
206 TONIGHT	*Blue Moves* (1976)
212 TRUE LOVE	*Duets* (1993)
218 WE ALL FALL IN LOVE SOMETIMES	*Captain Fantastic and the Brown Dirt Cowboy* (1975)
222 WHIPPING BOY	*Too Low for Zero* (1983)
228 WHISPERS	*Sleeping with the Past* (1989)
199 WHO WEARS THESE SHOES?	*Breaking Hearts* (1984)
232 A WORD IN SPANISH	*Reg Strikes Back* (1988)
238 WRAP HER UP	*Ice on Fire* (1985)
242 YOU CAN MAKE HISTORY (YOUNG AGAIN)	*Love Songs* (1996)
247 YOU GOTTA LOVE SOMEONE	*To Be Continued* (1990)
252 YOU'RE SO STATIC	*Caribou* (1974)
257 YOUR SISTER CAN'T TWIST (BUT SHE CAN ROCK 'N' ROLL)	*Goodbye Yellow Brick Road* (1973)
262 YOUR SONG	*Elton John* (1970)

LOVE LIES BLEEDING

Words and Music by ELTON JOHN
and BERNIE TAUPIN

MADMAN ACROSS THE WATER

Words and Music by ELTON JOHN
and BERNIE TAUPIN

The in-laws hope they'll see___ you ver - y soon._____

But is it in your con - science that you're af - ter

an-oth-er glimpse of the Mad-man A-cross The Wa - ter._____

Repeat and fade

LUCY IN THE SKY WITH DIAMONDS

Words and Music by JOHN LENNON
and PAUL McCARTNEY

Moderately

Pic - ture your -
Fol - low her
Pic - ture your -

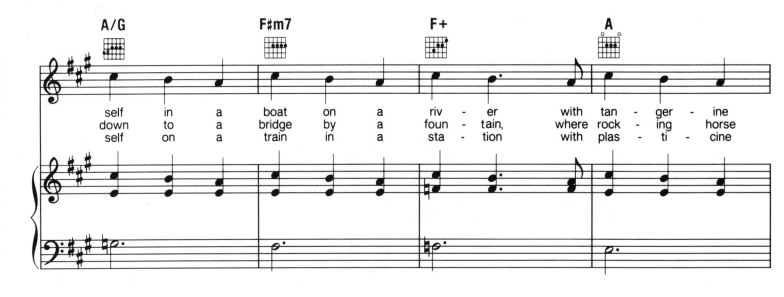

self in a boat on a riv - er with tan - ger - ine
down to a bridge by a foun - tain, where rock - ing horse
self on a train in a sta - tion with plas - ti - cine

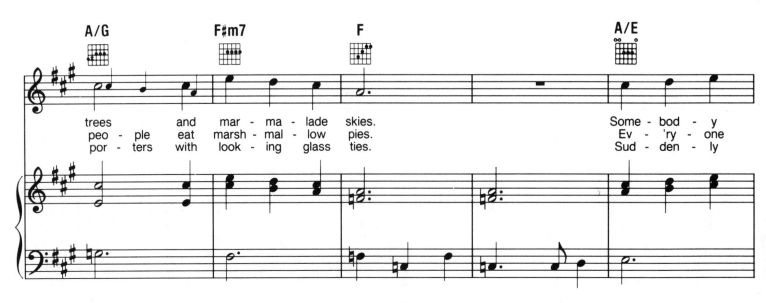

trees and mar - ma - lade skies. Some - bod - y
peo - ple eat marsh - mal - low pies. Ev - 'ry - one
por - ters with look - ing glass ties. Sud - den - ly

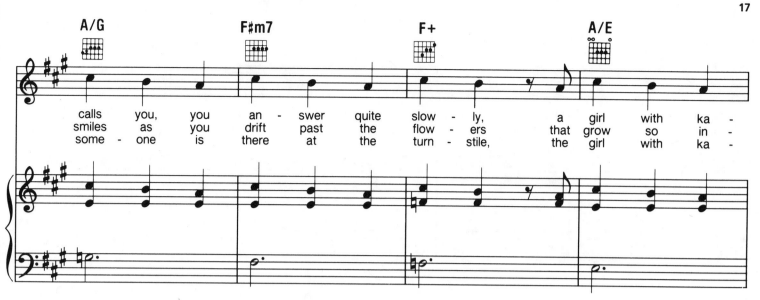

calls you, you an - swer quite slow - ly, a girl with ka -
smiles as you drift past the flow - ers that grow so in -
some - one is there at the turn - stile, the girl with ka -

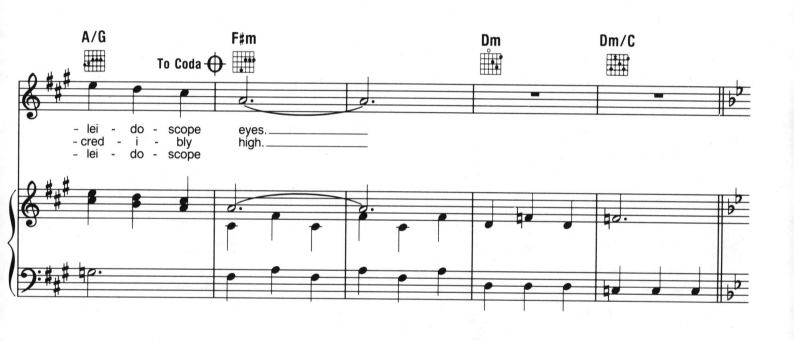

- lei - do - scope eyes.
- cred - i - bly high.
- lei - do - scope

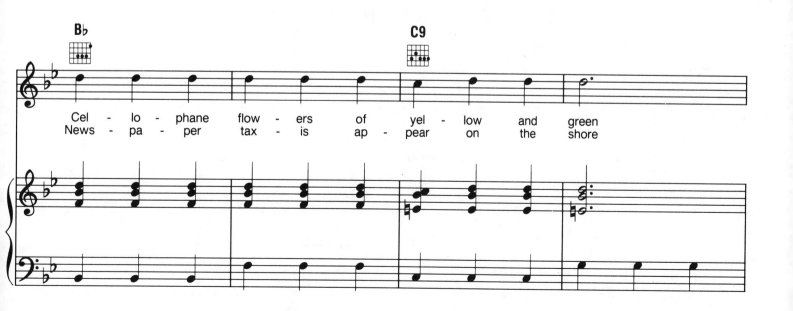

Cel - lo - phane flow - ers of yel - low and green
News - pa - per tax - is ap - pear on the shore

MADE IN ENGLAND

Words and Music by ELTON JOHN
and BERNIE TAUPIN

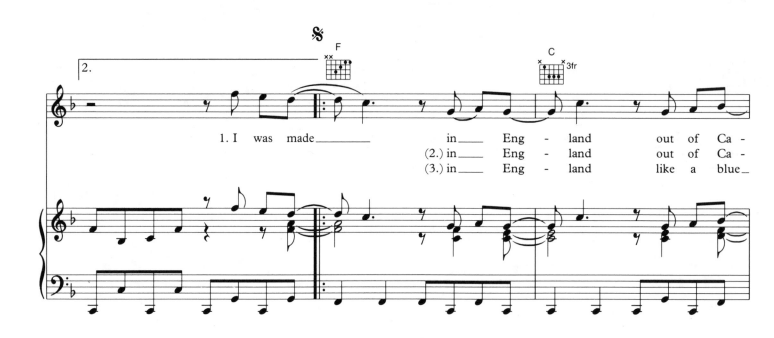

1. I was made _____ in _____ Eng - land out of Ca -
(2.) in _____ Eng - land out of Ca -
(3.) in _____ Eng - land like a blue _

- dil - lac mus - cle, I had a quit - me fa -
- dil - lac mus - cle, face down on a play -
_ Cor - ti - na, but a Yan - kee sum -

I was

made   in   Eng - land!

repeat ad lib. to fade

MADNESS

Words and Music by ELTON JOHN
and GARY OSBORNE

help - less   caught up in the   mad   -   ness   of a

world   gone   mad,   (Solo)

burn - ing in a blind man's eyes. And it's
hid - den in the hate and pain. There is
burn - ing in a wild man's brain. And it's
ev - 'ry time the bul - lets start. There is
burn ing in a poor man's heart.

Solo ad lib.

And it's

mad - ness ___ some-thing that we can't con - trol. There is
mad - ness ___ burn-ing in a blind man's soul.

4th time et seq.

To Fade

(mad - ness ___) (mad - ness ___) mad - ness. ___

MAMA CAN'T BUY YOU LOVE

Words and Music by LEROY BELL
and CASEY JAMES

1. Ba - by, ___ so they give you an - y - thing. ___
2. Ba- by, ___ fan - cy friends show you ___ a smile. ___

MEMORY OF LOVE

Words and Music by ELTON JOHN
and GARY OSBORNE

MICHELLE'S SONG
from the Motion Picture FRIENDS

Words and Music by ELTON JOHN
and BERNIE TAUPIN

1. Cast a peb-ble on — the wa-ter, watch the rip-ples gent-ly spread-ing, ti-ny
2. Sleep-ing in the o-pen, see the shad-ows soft-ly mov-ing, take a
(3.) learned to be so graceful watch-ing wild horses run-ning, and

daugh-ter of — the Cam-argue, we were meant to be — to-geth-er. ___
train to-wards the south-land, our time was never bet-ter. ___
from those agile an-gels, we knew the tide was turn-ing. ___

MONA LISAS AND MAD HATTERS

Words and Music by ELTON JOHN
and BERNIE TAUPIN

In a slow two

Now I know _____
This Broad-way's got _____

it's got a "Span-ish Har - lem" are ____ not

just I pret-ty words _____ to say.
if I know the tunes _____ I might _ join in. _____

NIKITA

Words and Music by ELTON JOHN
and BERNIE TAUPIN

Moderately

Hey, Nik - it - a, is it cold __ in your lit - tle corn - - er
Do you ev - er dream of me? __ Do you ev - er see the let - ters

of the world? You could roll a - round the globe, __
that I write? When you look up through the wire,

nev - er___ know.___

NO VALENTINES

Words and Music by ELTON JOHN
and BERNIE TAUPIN

NOBODY WINS

French Words and Music by JEAN-PAUL DREAU
English Words by GARY OSBORNE

THE ONE

Words and Music by ELTON JOHN
and BERNIE TAUPIN

(1.) I saw you danc-ing out_ the o-

cean,   run-ning fast __ a-long the sand,__

ba - by you're the one.

VERSE 2:
There are caravans we follow
Drunken nights in dark hotels,
When chances breathe between the silence
Where sex and love no longer gel.

For each man in his time is Cain
Until he walks along the beach
And sees his future in the water
A long lost heart within his reach.

ONE HORSE TOWN

Words and Music by ELTON JOHN,
BERNIE TAUPIN and JAMES NEWTON HOWARD

not a great deal of crime. ___

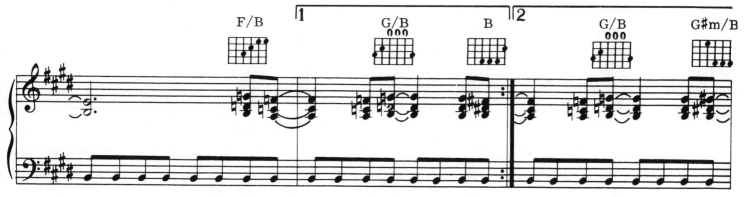

And they ain't too well ac - quaint-ed with the Stars and Stripes, —

But if you wan - na hear Sus - an - na then they'll pick all night,

D. S. al Coda|1

— They'll pick — all night. —

2. Sure is hell living in a one horse town,
Half a mile of Alabama mud bed ground.
Nothing much doing of an afternoon,
Unless you're sitting in a rocking chair
just picking a tune.

3. 'Cos it's no dice living in a one horse town,
Laid back, as my old coon hound.
And I just can't wait to get out of
this one horse town,
There's nothing to steal 'cos there's
simply nothing much around.

4. Sure is hell living in this one horse town,
Half a mile of Alabama mud bed ground.
And I just can't wait to grow out of
this one horse town,
There's nothing to steal 'cos there's
nothing much around.

PAIN

Words and Music by ELTON JOHN
and BERNIE TAUPIN

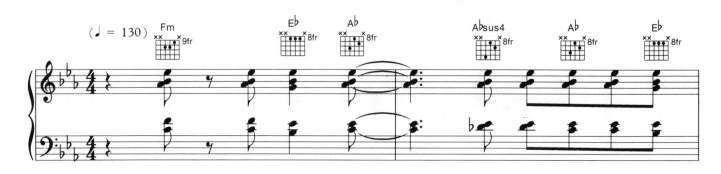

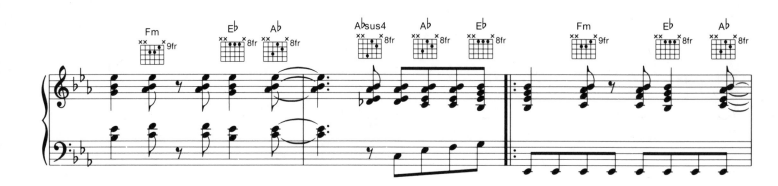

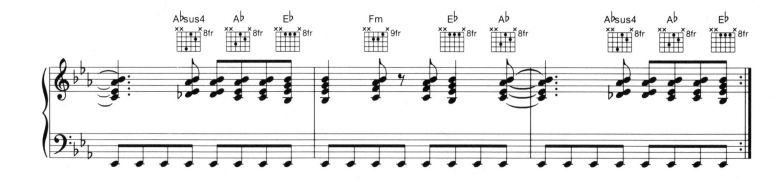

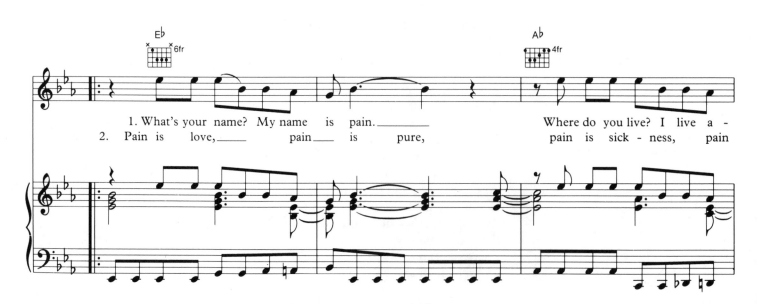

1. What's your name? My name is pain._____ Where do you live? I live a -
2. Pain is love,_____ pain__ is pure, pain is sick - ness, pain

I____ am pain.____

PART-TIME LOVE

Words and Music by ELTON JOHN
and GARY OSBORNE

PINBALL WIZARD

Words and Music by
PETER TOWNSHEND

1. Ev-er since I was a young boy___ I
   stands___ like a stat- ue,___ be-comes
   Ain't got no dis-trac-tions,___ can't
4. He's been on my fav-'rite tab- le,___

1.2. He's a pin - ball wiz - ard there has ___ to be a twist, A
3. I thought I was ___ the bod - y - ta - ble king, But

pin - ball wiz - ard, got such a sup - ple wrist ___
I just hand - ed my pin - ball crown to him. ___

1. 2.

How do you think ___ he does ___ it? ___
(I ___ don't ___ know. ___)

3.   D.S. al Coda

What makes him ___ so ___ good? ___
2. He
3. ___

Coda

ball.

PHILADELPHIA FREEDOM

Words and Music by ELTON JOHN
and BERNIE TAUPIN

Verse 2. If you choose to, you can live your life alone
Some people choose the city,
Some others choose the good old family home
I like living easy without family ties
'Til the whippoorwill of freedom zapped me
Right between the eyes

Repeat Chorus

PRINCESS

Words and Music by ELTON JOHN
and GARY OSBORNE

(3rd time—Instrumental solo)

Have-n't you heard___ what's new,_____

Have-n't you heard___ them say,_____

there is a

I was a

rum - our ___ go-ing a-round_ that sud-den-ly I've ___ found you.

pris-on - er, ___ bur-ied a-live_ now sud-den-ly I've ___ been freed.

You're my prin - cess, you're my prin - cess.

To Coda

D.%. al Coda

CODA

Repeat to fade

(Solo ad lib.)

RECOVER YOUR SOUL

Words and Music by ELTON JOHN
and BERNIE TAUPIN

ROCKET MAN
(I Think It's Gonna Be a Long Long Time)

Words and Music by ELTON JOHN
and BERNIE TAUPIN

To Coda

RUNAWAY TRAIN

Words and Music by ELTON JOHN,
BERNIE TAUPIN and OLLE ROMO

CODA

And I've poured out the pleas-sure and dealt with the pain, __ stand-ing in a sta-tion wait-ing in the rain. __ I'm start-ing to feel __ a lit-tle mus- cle a-gain __ but love is lost like a run-a-way __ train. __

Repeat to Fade

VERSE 2:
Well we've wrapped ourselves in golden crowns
Like sun gods spitting rain;
Found a way home written on this map
Like red dye in my veins.
In the hardest times that come around,
The fear of losing grows;
I've lost and seen the world shut down,
It's a darkness no one knows,

Oh. . .oh.

(D.S.)
Verse 3:
Instrumental
Oh. . .oh. . .mm

SAD SONGS
(Say So Much)

Words and Music by ELTON JOHN
and BERNIE TAUPIN

SACRIFICE

Words and Music by ELTON JOHN
and BERNIE TAUPIN

It's a hu-man sign _____ when things _ go wrong, _
Mu-tual mis-un-der-stand-ing af-ter the fact. _

_ when the scent of her lin - gers _____ and temp - ta-tion's strong. _
_ Sen - si - tiv - i - ty builds _ a pris - on in the fi - nal act. __

SARTORIAL ELOQUENCE

Words and Music by ELTON JOHN
and TOM ROBINSON

SATURDAY NIGHT'S ALRIGHT
(For Fighting)

Words and Music by ELTON JOHN
and BERNIE TAUPIN

With a beat

SHOOT DOWN THE MOON

Words and Music by ELTON JOHN
and BERNIE TAUPIN

SLEEPING WITH THE PAST

Words and Music by ELTON JOHN
and BERNIE TAUPIN

SIMPLE LIFE

Words and Music by ELTON JOHN
and BERNIE TAUPIN

VERSE

(1.) There's a break - down on the run - way and the time-
(2.) When we break __ out of this blind - fold Take__

- less flights __ are gone; ___ I'm a year ___ a - head ___ of my-self ___
__ you from __ this place; ___ un - til ____ we're free __ from this ball __

__ these days __ and I'm lo - co - mo - tive strong. ___ My ci -
__ and chain __ I'm still hard be - hind __ the eight. ___ My ci -

- ty spread like can - non fire ___ in a yel - low ner - vous state; __
- ty beats like ham - mered steel __ on a shal - low cru - el rock; __

bend, and with the last breath we ev - er take we're gon-na get back to the sim-

- ple life a - gain.

(Instr.)

D.S. Rpt. Chorus to Fade

1.

2.

And I won't

SIXTY YEARS ON

Words and Music by ELTON JOHN
and BERNIE TAUPIN

Who'll walk me down to church when I'm six - ty years of age,
You've hung up your great coat and you've laid down your gun,
Yes, I'll sit with you and talk, let your eyes re - live a - gain,

when the rag - ged dog they gave me has been ten years in the
you know the war you fought in was - n't too much
I know my vin - tage prayers will be ver - y much the

2.
Am
Bm
On.
G/A bass
A/B bass
D/A bass
E/B bass
C/A bass
D/B bass
Am
Bm
G/A bass
A/B bass
D/A bass
E/B bass
C/A bass
D/B bass
Am
Bm
D. S. al Coda

SKYLINE PIGEON

Words and Music by ELTON JOHN
and BERNIE TAUPIN

D. S. al Coda

all, please free me from this ach - ing met - al ring, and

Coda

things you left so ver - y, so ver - y

far _____ be - hind. _____

SOMEONE SAVED MY LIFE TONIGHT

Words and Music by ELTON JOHN
and BERNIE TAUPIN

Verse 2. I never realized the passing hours
Of evening showers,
A slip noose hanging in my darkest dreams.
I'm strangled by your haunted social scene
Just a pawn out-played by a dominating queen.
It's four-o-clock in the morning
Damn it!
Listen to me good.
I'm sleeping with myself tonight
Saved in time, thank God my music's still alive.

To Chorus

SOMETHING ABOUT THE WAY YOU LOOK TONIGHT

Words and Music by ELTON JOHN
and BERNIE TAUPIN

Original Key: F-sharp major. This edition has been transposed down one half-step to be more playable.

SONG FOR GUY

By ELTON JOHN

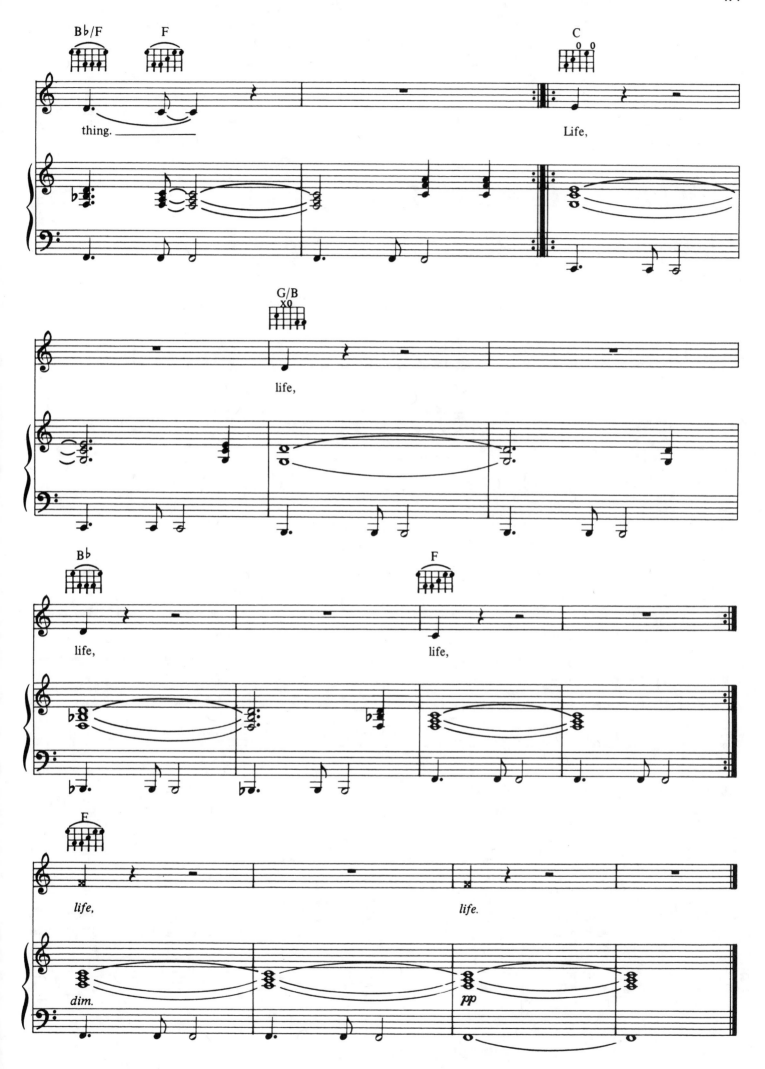

SORRY SEEMS TO BE THE HARDEST WORD

Words and Music by ELTON JOHN
and BERNIE TAUPIN

What have I got to do to make you love me

What have I got to do to make you care.

What do I do when light-ning strikes me

And I wake to find that you're not there

STEP INTO CHRISTMAS

Words and Music by ELTON JOHN
and BERNIE TAUPIN

Wel-come to___ my Christ-mas song,___ I'd like to thank you for___

the__ year._____ So I'm a-

send - ing you__ this Christ - mas card_____ to say it's nice to have___

__ you__ here._____

I'd like to sing a - bout all__ the things_ your eyes and mine_ can see,__

come a - long with me, step in - to Christ - mas, the ad - mis - sion's free.

next year, and keep smil - ing through the days.

Take care in all you do

If we can help to en -

SWEET PAINTED LADY

Words and Music by ELTON JOHN
and BERNIE TAUPIN

TAKE ME TO THE PILOT

Words and Music by ELTON JOHN
and BERNIE TAUPIN

TEACHER I NEED YOU

Words and Music by ELTON JOHN
and BERNIE TAUPIN

TINY DANCER

Words and Music by ELTON JOHN
and BERNIE TAUPIN

WHO WEARS THESE SHOES?

Words and Music by ELTON JOHN
and BERNIE TAUPIN

There's a light

TONIGHT

Words and Music by ELTON JOHN
and BERNIE TAUPIN

TRUE LOVE
from HIGH SOCIETY

Words and Music by
COLE PORTER

WE ALL FALL IN LOVE SOMETIMES

Words and Music by ELTON JOHN
and BERNIE TAUPIN

Did we, didn't we, should we, couldn't we I'm not sure 'cause some-times we're so blind Strug-gling through the day

when ev-en your best friend says___ Don't you find___

___ We all fall in love some - times___

Piano guide

Solo ad lib.

220

WHIPPING BOY

Words and Music by ELTON JOHN
and BERNIE TAUPIN

To Coda ⊕

won't be ____ your whip-ping ____ boy. ____

ooh ____

ooh ____

It's this il -

WHISPERS

Words and Music by ELTON JOHN
and BERNIE TAUPIN

1. Look at me twice__ with the wild cat - eyes__ Pro - mise me ev - ery-thing Ex -
(2.) -mount to a lie__ with__ linger - ing breath Walk-ing fing - ers run hung - ry

-cept a blue night__ Shud - der like ice__ in cut crys - tal glass__
scrat - ches left__ Dull chimes ring - ing like an em - pty voice__ A

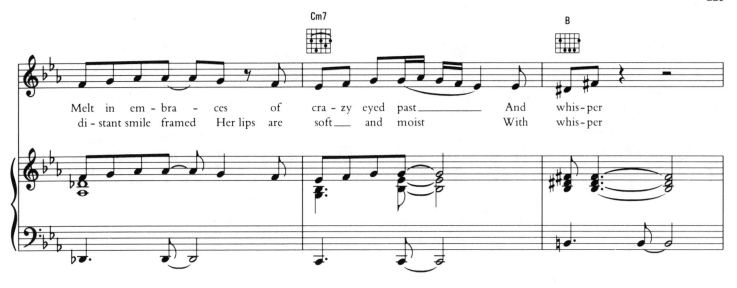

Melt in em- bra- ces of cra - zy eyed past_____ And whis- per
di - stant smile framed Her lips are soft___ and moist With whis- per

whis- per whis- per-ing whis - pers__
whis- per whis- per-ing whis - pers__

2. Tan-ta - And

Chorus: *first time without repeats*
        second time with repeats

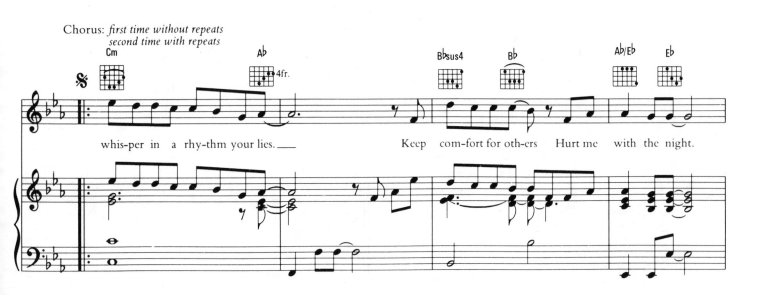

whis- per in a rhy- thm your lies.__ Keep com-fort for oth-ers Hurt me with the night.

Whis-per like cold winds Close to the bone___ Save hea-ven for lov-ers Leave

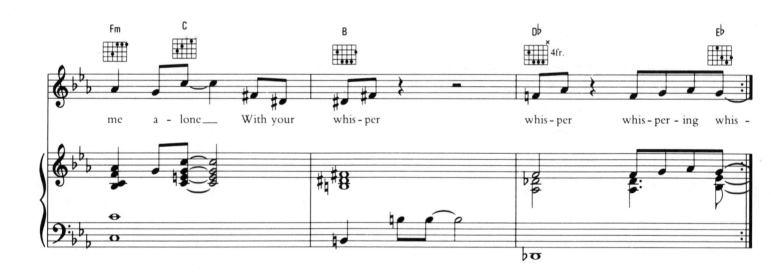

me a - lone___ With your whis-per whis-per whis-per-ing whis-

- pers_____ (2.)__ pers_____

A WORD IN SPANISH

Words and Music by ELTON JOHN
and BERNIE TAUPIN

Moderately slow

I don't know why, you can't com-pre-hend,

I just know I do, read it in my eyes. I just can't ex-plain in this

If you don't un-der-stand it's love

WRAP HER UP

Words and Music by ELTON JOHN, BERNIE TAUPIN, DAVEY JOHNSTONE,
CHARLIE MORGAN, PAUL WESTWOOD and FRED MANDEL

___and beau - ties but they all can dance. Wrap her up, I'll take her

home with me, wrap her up, she is all I need, wrap her

up

1.
give her to me, wrap her up.___
Is she

2. *D.S. AD LIB. TO FADE*
give her to me wrap her up.___
Wrap her

YOU CAN MAKE HISTORY
(Young Again)

Words and Music by ELTON JOHN
and BERNIE TAUPIN

Moderately, expressively

I can feel the time
I can watch the weeks

clos - ing in. I can feel the years crawl - ing through my skin.___ And if I
sweep - ing by. I can re - col - lect the hearts hang - ing out to dry.___ When the

doubt my - self,___ I can count on the rain ___ to
world shuts down,___ I can touch my fears.___ I can

YOU GOTTA LOVE SOMEONE

featured in the Paramount Motion Picture DAYS OF THUNDER

Words and Music by ELTON JOHN
and BERNIE TAUPIN

YOU'RE SO STATIC

Words and Music by ELTON JOHN
and BERNIE TAUPIN

YOUR SISTER CAN'T TWIST
(But She Can Rock 'n' Roll)

Words and Music by ELTON JOHN
and BERNIE TAUPIN

YOUR SONG

Words and Music by ELTON JOHN
and BERNIE TAUPIN